Cap'n Jimbo

Dedicated to Marie...My Best Friend

Cap'n Jimbo

By Jimbo Chapman, AKC
As related to Roger Chapman

Robert D. Reed Publishers • San Francisco, California

Robert D. Reed Publishers
750 La Playa Street, Suite 647
San Francisco, CA 94121
Phone: 650-994-6570 • Fax: -6579
E-mail: 4bobreed@msn.com
Web site: www.rdrpublishers.com

Editor: **Ruth Schenkel**
Cover Designer: **Julia A. Gaskill**
Photographers: **Roger Chapman and Marie Chapman**

ISBN 1-885003-90-0
Library of Congress Control Number 2001088123

Manufactured, Typeset, and Printed in the United States

PHOTOGRAPHS

Cap'n Jimbo Chapman	Cover
Dedicated to Marie.My Best Friend	ii
First Night on Wild Goose Point	9
Marie and Jimbo. Narragansett Beach Rhode Island	11
Follow the Yellow Markers...	11
Nemo Melhorn	18
Jimbo and Nemo Enjoying A Victory Lunch	19
Well, There Goes Wickford	26
Jimbo and Friend Aboard Sea Shanty	27
Lunch Time Aboard Sea Shanty	28
Sea Legs at Last	29
Boy! This Is A Long Watch	30
Can't We Take A Short Break?	31
Nancy, Jimbo and John Having A Field Day	33
The Best Walks Are with John and His Dogs	34
Heidi Looking For Jimbo on Rome Point, Rhode Island	34
After A Long Day in the Field A Short Nap is in Order	35
Father Jimbo Chapman	38
New Kid On The Plat	42
Trick or Treat	43
Jimbo's Very Own English Sports Car	49
Cap'n Jimbo Chapman 1955-1969	66

Photographs by Roger Chapman

CONTENTS

List of Photographs   iv
Preface   vii
Chapter One   Now I Shall Write My Autobiography   1
Chapter Two   And We Were Just Going Look at the Puppies   3
Chapter Three   First Night on Wild Goose Point   7
Chapter Four   Sore Paw   13
Chapter Five   Enter Nemo   17
Chapter Six   Let's Go Sailing Jimbo   21
Chapter Seven   A Field Day   31
Chapter Eight   Father Jimbo   37
Chapter Nine   Trick or Treat   41
Chapter Ten   The MG TD and the Roastbeef   47
Chapter Eleven   Doctor Kind   53
Chapter Twelve   Jimbo! I Think That I Heard You Speak   57
Chapter Thirteen   We Didn't Mean to Hurt Him Lady   59
Epilogue   67
About the Author   68
About the Ghostwriter   68

PREFACE

The first several chapters of this story were written in the late Sixties. Our life suddenly became filled to the brim. The pages were punched and placed in a three-ring notebook. For more than thirty years the blue imitation-leather cover stared down at me from the third shelf of the bookcase next to my desk. Last fall I took it down and read the first few chapters. Today I wrote the final chapter.

Perhaps a story told by a Springer Spaniel will not appeal to some, but *Cap'n Jimbo* became such an important part of our lives that his antics and busy life might be worth passing on. Or at least be labeled and returned to the third shelf, a complete and legible legacy available to those who have loved a Springer Spaniel.

Roger Chapman
September 2000

CHAPTER ONE

Now I shall write my autobiography...

In this changing world of space travel and Gravy Train, an autobiography by a member of the canine race may not come as a complete surprise. But I have made a major breakthrough in a little known science of communication between man and *canis familiaris.* Although I cannot entirely disclose my findings, what you are about to read is without a doubt a Fido first– living proof of a great modern discovery. This hairy tale may swing to and fro with little rhyme or reason and at times droop to a new literary low, but please bear in mind that this is the first such undertaking by a Springer Spaniel working through a rather dense medium.

And what about the medium? He is none other than my unsuspecting foster parent, Ole Rog. He is entirely unaware that he has been chosen as the liaison for this project and he thinks that the whole thing is his undertaking.

It all started early last spring. We were two days into the first spring nor'easter. Ole Rog, distraught and lost for things to do had retired to the "Hole." (The Hole is an underground darkroom, studio, electronics lab, guest room, laundry, heating plant and literary workshop.)

The time was right for himself to begin another of his two-page books. As he cranked the first eight-and-a-half-by-eleven page into the ancient Remington, I stretched my hind legs out and waited for the coolness of the basement floor to soothe my overtaxed stomach. (I really must concentrate on eating less!) A routine rest period appeared to be in order, but before I could construct an appropriate dream scene a strange and mystic mist filled the quiet space between Rog and me. The single lamp above the naked manuscript page seemed to be the only force holding us suspended in a faraway and totally darkened cosmos.

All at once I knew that I had found the secret that could break the sound barrier between man and his best friend. I must work fast and put it to the test, lest the nor'easter extinguishes the lamp and we fall back into the "Hole."

Suddenly, the Remington began to speak! *"CAP'N JIMBO"* appeared at the top of the lighted sheet of paper. By George, it works! Now I shall write my autobiography...

CHAPTER TWO

Just Going To Look At The Puppies...

A cold snow-laden wind had labored most of the day to blanket the noble Volkswagen standing just outside its warm and cozy bedroom. But it would not be long before the last of the eleven little guests would leave the garage and the little German could once again be sheltered from Vermont's winter perils.

As I think back to that cold and bitter evening in January 1956, I smile to myself, for even then, at just six weeks old, I must have possessed an unusual intuition. My mother, Ruthie's Run, had just finished giving the remaining five of us our supper. I cuddled up next to the runt to keep him warm and settled down for a good night's rest. But sleep wouldn't come. Gathering my thoughts, which had wandered around the garage, I tried to decide what the future held for "number five." (For the present, we were named according to the order of arrival.) Suddenly, I was wide awake with anxiety! It will happen tonight. I will leave mother and the others. My emotions were mixed with sadness and enchantment as I lay there waiting for whatever the night might bring.

Within the hour, I heard the stamping of feet and muffled greetings at the front door of the house. I slipped quietly away from the runt, squeezed through the secret opening of our enclosure and pressed my ear to the kitchen door. Apparently the new arrivals were old friends of mother's foster parents, Jimbo and Audrey Conniff, for there was a good deal of talk about Aspen where mother was born. They made their way to the coffee pot in the kitchen and I heard the one called Marie say, "We just stopped by to see the puppies if it isn't too late." Someone else said, "Okay" and in spite of the slight delay caused by the narrowness of the secret opening, I returned to my post in plenty of time. The kitchen door opened, letting in a wedge of bright light, a few bars of Chopin from the new hi-fi, the wonderful aroma of freshly brewed coffee, and four hushed voices. (And what, you may ask, would a six week old puppy know about an invisible emanation created by brewing coffee? Nothing. But, in my later years I learned to appreciate a good saucer of coffee blended with just the right amount of real heavy cream.)

The door closed and the overhead light took the place of the wedge that had already forced its way into the sleepy eyes of the others. Everyone was up by the time the foursome arrived at the enclosure. But I played it cool. No sense rushing things. I'll just rest while they shop around. (Not one of them thought to bring even a morsel of food.)

The runt was the first to be inspected. There was much ado over him until someone mentioned the word "runt." He was quickly exchanged for Mister Seven. (This may have been my first lesson in sociology. Beware of a status symbol. Once established you have to live up to it or live it down.) Two other puppies were selected for appraisal and I distinctly recall the act that Mister Six ran through. It was so well done that I was forced to put aside my pride and enter into the action.

It appeared, however, that my decision was made just a little too late, for Mister Six was making his curtain call before I could get underway. In desperation, I filled the air with soft puppy sounds and turned my sad eyes toward the quiet one in the knickers. (In time, you will learn that Rog is a rather odd duck who wears knickers when skiing and shaves with an old fashioned straight-edge razor. Like most men he has very little to say about such things as purchasing puppy dogs or other domestic commodities.) I watched as Mister Six licked the face of the fair lady called Marie as she carried him all the way to the kitchen door. The click of the overhead light switch was as final as the darkness that returned to the garage and my heart. I was devastated.

It is difficult to recall how much time passed or just how much rationalizing I did before I heard the voices returning to the door of our room. I shall never forget the joy that filled me for I felt sure that the skiing puppy shoppers had realized their mistake and were coming to get me instead of Mister Six. But, no! They were simply returning him to the enclosure while they finished their coffee. Oh well, I thought, forget the whole thing and try to get some sleep. After all, they weren't very nice. And besides, what kind of a life would it be living with a couple of oddball skiers who are so prone to snap judgment? Really, I might end up in some cold, out-of-the-way mountain pass toting an oversize rucksack, or I could spend countless weekends confined to a frigid station wagon stranded in an isolated parking lot. To say nothing about what the fools might do during the summer months.

The reader may wonder how a very young Springer Spaniel who had never left the confines of his Perkinsville, Vermont bedroom could know so much about skiers. Well, the quaint old house was so often filled with family, friends and even just off-the-slope freeloaders. Skiers all! Each one bent on reliving every run down ski trails from Vermont to Colorado. I listened to every one of these exciting episodes. I heard about Rene's Chalet Where The Poodles Stay, and the nice old man at the parking lot at Aspen who will, for a buck, knock on the Mercedes window every hour to prevent Lovable Louie from freezing to the stiff leather back seat. Yes sir, I know all about that breed!

Relieved that I had been spared such a life, I nestled

quietly against the runt. My mind was clear and open. I began to slip into the wonders of the subconscious universe. (Puppies dream too, you, know!)

There they were, knickers and all, hovering over me. Marie's red hair hung between her outstretched arms.

"I think that this is the one," filtered into my misty mind as I floated up out of the enclosure and into a very warm and dark place. Everything around me, was soft and smelled so different. (The runt was never like this!) Wherever my dream had taken me I was so very comfortable. But what had happened to the guy in the knickers? It was so strange. I could hear their whispered voices, Marie's so near and his so distant. Soon, my comfortable niche became mobile. Are their voices to haunt me forever? Why can't I see them? How I wished that I could awaken and return to mother and the others. Instead, the dream faded leaving only a nice sweet odor and the best sleep since my arrival to this crazy planet.

I must be awake! Where am I? What is that strange sound under me? And why am I all wrapped up in this fuzzy thing? I better not move until I figure out the situation. Perhaps we are on the way to the vet for some of those awful shots that everyone has been talking about. But where are the others? No! This is different. I hear Rog and Marie again.

"And we were just going to *look* at the puppies. I guess that the gang at Mad River won the bet! Do you think that we should have taken him, Rog?"

"Of course! After all, your family has a history of great dogs. Why should it stop with you? And besides, I like him."

"So do I. Wonder when he will wake up. You'd think that poor little guy would have to piddle."

"Maybe he has!"

CHAPTER THREE

First night on Wild Goose Point...

The long journey from Perkinsville,Vermont to Wickford, Rhode Island, was uneventful and quiet with only one gas and coffee fill-up stop. I, of course, was accompanied to a nearby shoveled area whereupon I demonstrated my limited toilet training. Once again the station wagon bumped its way toward my new home. I was gently covered with that fuzzy thing and placed upon Marie's lap.

Can it be that I'm theirs now? They must have mistaken me for Mister Six. Then it wasn't a dream! That sweet smell was perfume and the soft warm place...well, I'll be dammed. Maybe this isn't going to be so bad after all. Better plan a grandiose entrance pretty soon. Let's see, what would go over big with these funny bunnies? How about the face licking routine? No. Too mushy and she might have a cold. Maybe the whimpering act would get to her? But then, he may be the rough type and I'd end up on the floor in the back of this huge ice box they call a station wagon. If I knew just how far we were going I could play the good puppy bit and just stay right here for the whole trip. Let's go with that. And if it turns out that I don't like them, I'll switch to the bad dog routine. About two days of that and I'm back with Mom and the kids...

"You know Rog, I think that this little guy is a fast learner. All I had to do was put him down in the cleared area and he did his business all by himself."

Marie, it's no big deal. I did that all the time in the garage. What you don't know is that once I even lifted my leg and sent a short burst through the wire side of our room. Jim and Audrey saw the early childhood advancement and bragged about it for a week. I do wish that Marie could hear me, too.   Perhaps the inter-race communication project could be modified to include her. I'll work on it.

A strange sense of arrival awoke me as the station wagon made a slow turn and stopped just in front of a small shingled garage. Rog got out of the station wagon, opened the garage door, slipped back into the car and drove in. Am I destined to live my entire time on earth moving from one garage to another?

My new and enchanted life by the sea was about to begin. Marie opened the car door until it bumped against the wall and we squeezed out into the Rhode Island dampness. Well, at least there's no room for a pen in this tiny garage!

We scurried through the small rear door of the garage and then to the front door of a rather small cottage.

"Stay here for a moment while I turn on a few lights," Marie whispered, as she lowered me to the floor.

Somewhere a lamp came alive and I found myself in the center of a tiny living room. Not bad! Cozy and it smells like they use the fireplace. I'll adjust.

Rog arrived with a load of skiing gear and sundry other items.

"Where's Jimbo's springer? Has he wet on the rug yet?" was his opening line.

I don't think he has a very good feeling about sharing his castle with a puppy. And, no! I haven't wet the rug yet.

"He's on the kitchen couch still wrapped up in his blanket. Jimbo's springer. That sounds neat. Let's call him 'Jimbo'." Marie replied.

"If he's going to live by the sea and probably sail, why not call him Cap'n Jimbo?" Rog suggested.

"Okay. Little guy on the couch, from here on in you are officially called, *Cap'n Jimbo Chapman,*" Marie proclaimed.

So that's it. We live by the sea and sooner or later I'll probably end up in a wooden box with a pointy end, bouncing from wave to wave. Where is it written that a water spaniel is required to sail? All the Certificate of Pedigree says is, "English Springer Spaniel, Liver and White, Male and Date of Birth Nov. 27, 1955.

After a short trip into the bitter cold yard, Marie and I returned to the nice warm kitchen.

"There. He's all set for the night. Wonder where he should sleep?" Marie asked Rog.

"It would be too cold in the bedroom with the window open. Why not make him a bed in the corner? It's always warm there."

Now there's a guy after my heart. I'm beginning to like

First Night on Wild Goose Point

this arrangement.

"I'll get the loden coat. It's all soft wool and large enough to make a nice nest," Marie replied.

"Better put out a small cup of water and break up one of those puppy bones you bought to feed the sea gull," Rog suggested.

He's okay. I may have to like him after all. Can't wait to see what he looks like without those knickers. Maybe I could teach him something about the great outdoors.

The night went pretty well but I just made it to daybreak. Don't they know that puppies have to relieve the pressure about every two hours? And I really think Rog could be trained. I led him around the house twice before he caught on.

Wow! What a place to run and swim. The sea is about twenty feet from the house and there's a stairway down to the beach that will be a challenge. But my legs will grow fast and that will be conquered. Here it is, only my first day and already I like it.

Marie presented me with an instant breakfast of milk and some sort of cereal. Great! But I'm certain that after my first visit to the local vet they will switch me to some expensive concoction designed by a doggie dietitian to produce a profit from all the beef waste unfit for human consumption. Tomorrow I will concentrate on a "beg at the table" routine that will be subtle but effective. I'll start with Rog. He is of German descent and indubitably a meat lover. (Amazing how my vocabulary is improving with every day...)

Judging from all the talk about aircraft carriers and flying, Rog must have a job at the nearby Naval Station. Off he goes. Now I have Marie all to myself. If I stay here in my "loden nest" silent and relaxed while she does her chores, there will be time to plan my day.

It appears to be a nice day, perhaps we will play around the yard. I'll push for a short walk along the beach. I don't think there is a leash in the house, so I will just stand around until Marie makes her first move. Not a bad time to practice that heel

Marie and Jimbo, Narragansett Beach, Rhode Island

Follow The Yellow Markers and Wait For Us At The Top Of That Hill

routine that mother does so well. As I remember, at the "heel" command she just took a position a few steps behind Audrey, adjusted to her cadence and followed along. In view of my tender age, I'll not be given the heel command, but just imagine the wonderful words of praise that will fill the house when Rog returns tonight.

"And do you know that Jimbo heeled without a word. How in the world did he learn that?"

Why doesn't the pedigree stress the intellectual excellence of our breed?

Spring turned Marie's carefully placed seeds into a maze of colors that stopped a few passing cars and all the walkers. My short little legs lengthened and grew strong, ready to endure any adventurous hike Rog and Marie introduced. I must say that these guys are kind to animals. Often, Rog will stop, open wide the top of his Army surplus ski troop rucksack, gently slide me down to the towel padded bottom, and hoist the rucksack up onto his back. When I had rested enough, Marie will loosen the top, lift me out, and off I go again. Those memorable times in the New England woods, the sandy beach in Narragansett, or the tall grass on Beavertail were the best part of growing up. I do wish that the runt could have been with me.

CHAPTER FOUR

Sore paw...

My first summer on Wild Goose Point was indeed a wonderful learning experience. I learned to bark, swim, dive for rocks, discreetly beg at the table, find a nice warm place in their big bed on a cold night, and a few things I should not disclose.

Probably the most important discovery I made that summer was that I had the uncanny ability to win in a game of chance. My new talent had nothing to do with poker, dice or playing the numbers game. Very few humans can match my quickness and precision in the game I developed by chance. "Sore Paw" is perhaps nonexistent beyond the confines of my home but the game was extremely popular during the early 1960's. The reader may be interested in the origin of Sore Paw, so I will briefly review the history of the game.

One warm afternoon, Marie and I were playing rather hard on our rocky beach. I must have run across a sharp sea shell somewhere along the way that cut the large pad on my left paw. Marie rushed me up into the kitchen, cleaned and bandaged my wound while repeatedly uttering, "Jimbo, let me see your sore paw," and "Poor Jimbo has a sore paw." I appreciated her concern, but I must say that the sore paw baby-talk routine was a little annoying. After several minutes of this rather childish lamenting, I turned up my lip and uttered a muffled snarl. At first, Marie was alarmed. In an effort to soothe the situation, she said, "Okay Jimbo, we'll leave your sore paw alone." Sore paw again! I'll fix that! This time I gave her another snarl followed immediately by a near miss tooth clashing snap at her hand.

"We'll have none of that around here, Mister Jimbo Chapman!" said Marie, and followed with a quick right to my jaw. Of course, Marie had no way of knowing that the near miss was intentional and since her softened punch was more for show than for harm, no damage was done. But somehow this incident initiated the famous game of Sore Paw.

In time,most of the characters that hung around the Chapman kitchen challenged me to at least one game of Sore Paw. Usually, I would be hanging around the kitchen minding my own business when someone would sneak up, grab my left paw and utter, "Does poor Jimbo have a sore paw?" And in reply I would give them the standard lip curl followed with a growl and then a precision near miss snap. It was so difficult to adhere to my secret oath not to go the limit with the snap routine. But this was my side of the sore paw game someone, someday will find out just how quick and accurate ole Cap'n Jimbo can be.

I had pretty much selected my biggest competitor, Charlie Melhorn as the recipient of a right on target attack. Not because Charlie was a mean person, but just because he really thought he was master of the game. Each time we entered combat, I would strike just a little nearer to the mark. "Another win!" he would boast to all present. Charlie would glow with the aura of a knight carrying out the queen's wishes and announce, "Too bad, Jimbo. Maybe next time."

Perhaps this was a natural reaction for a man with such a grand military background. The son of an admiral, Charlie was an excellent pilot in the U.S. Navy with an honorable war record who was always ready for combat. Be it with an aggressive enemy aviator in a foreign sky or with a crafty Springer Spaniel waiting for him to make his first mistake, Charlie had to win. Stand by Commander.

Executive Officer Melhorn received TAD (Temporary Additional Duty) orders to the West Coast. I had one more session of Sore Paw left. Charlie arrived in our kitchen decked out in his best dress blues complete with sword and scrambled eggs hat. He was on the way to the squadron's final formation before the TAD group was to leave NAS Quonset Point Naval Station.

"Hi Jimbo. Thought I'd just stop in to say goodbye and have one last game of Sore Paw."

Too bad commander. This time you lose, were my final thoughts...

The players maneuvered to their customary positions. The Springer Spaniel under the kitchen table and the XO lying on the floor, ready for the final challenge. Complete silence descended upon the kitchen.

"Has poor ole Jimbo got a sore paw?"

I changed tactics. The lip curl and snarl were eliminated and I went directly to the snap. Charlie pulled back his wounded hand and said, "I guess you won this time Jimbo."

I slowly came out from under the table and sat down beside my friend. Winning was not important anymore. How I wished that I had lost again. In an effort to recoup whatever friendship that remained, I softly leaned against his leg. Charlie must have understood the gesture. He washed and wiped his hand with a paper towel that Marie handed him, patted my head and said, "You're faster than I thought ole boy. So long. I'll send you a postcard wherever I stop along the way. Take care."

I received several postcards sent from various naval air stations where he and his AD-5 aircraft RON'ed (Remain Over Night). Each contained a smart aleck message signed by Yogi Berra. The messages became more meaningful after I learned that baseball catcher's mitts are made out of dog hide.

CHAPTER FIVE

Enter Nemo...

Long before the sore paw incident, I happened on to a friendly neighborhood shaggy dog. Although the meeting was not as formal as I would have liked, he, who was called Nemo, became my best canine buddy.

I had reached the point on my learning curve where I was allowed to roam loose within the confines of my beautiful yard on Wild Goose Point.   Actually, I think that it was a difficult module in my toilet training program that prompted Marie to grant this early autonomy.

"Rog, I don't think Jimbo will ever learn to lift his leg!"

I, too, had given up. In desperation, I'd just squat; I rationalized that in time it would happen.

While I was enjoying the relief of my early morning emergency squat, I sensed that someone was watching. From over my shoulder, a rather strange voice said,

"At first I thought you were a girl. Someone has to teach you how to do it like a guy. Guys lift their leg in a dignified matter at times like this."

"I know all that, but how in the world do you do it? And who are you?"

Nemo Melhorn

"I'm Nemo Melhorn from a few doors north of here. I live with Commander and Jackie Melhorn, Navy people," was his reply. "Now let's get on with the program.

See that maple over there in the center of the lawn? Follow me.

"When I was your age I had no one to teach me and it came hard. I toppled over every time until I lucked out one day during a practice shot. Instead of toppling over this time, I fell against the tree. As a matter of fact, it was this very tree. Tasteful guys never lift their leg in their own yard. At that very moment, I realized that the operation was nothing more than a matter of precision balance. It's kind of like making a perfect 3-point landing in a tail dragger. But you're too young for me to get into that."

Nemo maneuvered me very close to the maple and said, "Now just lean against the tree and try lifting your outside rear leg. I know that it's hard to do but that's the whole point of leaning against the tree. Next, I want you to adjust the other three legs until you find the exact balance point where you do not need the support of the tree. It takes awhile, but once you find that point, you're there!"

I labored with his unpretentious description for several minutes. All at once, I hit the exact stance, gently moved away from the maple, and there it was, just as advertised! In the excitement of the moment and without warning, the basic purpose of the mission was accomplished. Not a drop hit my shaking outstretched leg!

"You're a fast learner, kid. There are a lot of neat things I will teach you, if you like," Nemo proudly stated.

I really like this guy. We will have fun together.

Marie arrived and said, "I see you've met Nemo. He's the best dog on the plat. You'll be good together. But Jackie doesn't like for him to come here. I think that she knows we give him goodies once in a while."

In a short time, I nonchalantly walked over to the maple, demonstrated the standard toilet procedure practiced by dignified men throughout the canine world and returned to Marie's side.

"Jimbo Chapman! Did Nemo teach you that?" she

Jimbo And Nemo Enjoying A Victory Lunch

laughed and patted Nemo on his curly head. "Good boy, Nemo."

In the months that followed, Nemo and I developed a meeting routine. Since Jackie had tightened up on Nemo's roaming radius, our meetings had to be discreet and out of sight. The not-in-the-house rule was reinforced to the point where Marie was forced to enter the game.

The "Don't you let Nemo in your house again!" quote from Jackie slowly became the front yard clich`e.

On a lazy afternoon, I was waiting for Nemo under the maple tree. Marie wandered over and asked, "What has happened to Nemo? He's rather late isn't he?"

"I don't really know, but I think he's depressed. You know how much he likes to come down here. And now he can't come in the house!" I answered, even though I knew that Marie could not hear me.

Marie looked at me in a strange way and said, "Let me think about it for a while." and slowly walked away.

The next day, shortly before Nemo's usual arrival time, Marie brought our short homemade ladder over from the garage. Its wide board steps and the incline angle, when placed under the window on the ocean side of the house, provided a perfect doggie access to the kitchen.

"Now, Jimbo, here's what we are going to do. When Nemo comes, get him over here as soon as possible. Tell him to climb the ladder," Marie directed.

As commanded, we adhered to the rule, "Don't you let Nemo in your house again!" Nemo did it all on his own.

He and Jimbo sat at the kitchen table to enjoy a special victory meal prepared by the lady of the house. The event passed and not a word was mentioned beyond the boundaries of our yard. But it must be noted that great laughter and applause filled our kitchen for many years whenever the episode came to light.

CHAPTER SIX

Let's go sailing Jimbo

Today, I learned that we are to have a new sailboat. I really don't know what my part will be in this new venture but it sounds pretty interesting. Perhaps a review of what has transpired in the Chapman sailing world would be enlightening.

When I arrived on the scene, they introduced me to *Old Dad* (later on I called it *Old Dam*), a fat little twelve foot crossbreed mixture of a Wood Pussy and a catboat. Now isn't that typical? Here I am a thoroughbred Springer Spaniel with a pedigree as long as your arm, being asked to enter a sailing career in the smallest, most bizarre looking vessel on all of Narragansett Bay. And, of course, there was no way out. I'd be much more comfortable recovering a fallen duck in some remote back bay cove than trying to learn the meaning of starboard, wind line, heel, luffing and all that maritime lingo— but you do what you have to do. At least I would be on the water, or more likely in it most of the time with these two birds in command. Nevertheless, I endured the summer in *Old Dam* and even looked forward to the call to action, "Let's go sailing Jimbo." Most of all, I enjoyed the trips to Fox Island. The island is about

750 yards due east from our beach and about a two hour sail in *Old Dad.*

Mr. and Mrs. Prew lived on Fox Island during the summer months and I think they liked dogs. Often we would stay for supper and watch television. (It was bad for a puppy to watch TV, so we didn't have one at home.) If the wind had died, Hap would launch the big power boat and tow us to our mooring. The three of us would laugh and play all the way to the beach, take an outside shower, and hop into bed.

One evening, the five of us were sitting around the supper table on the island when Hap said, "You guys ought to have a better boat. One day soon I'll gather up all the parts left from our National One Design and we'll take them over to Al Potter. He'll build you a nice boat." And that he did! Even I loved the rig when it was finished. Rog and Marie loved it so much that Rog wrote *Over And Out,* a photo-narrative of her building.

Watching a boat happen in an old barn filled with piles of nice soft cedar chips, a warm pot belly stove and ready source of goodies from Fredia's kitchen, was an adventure. Even for a Springer.

We sailed *Over And Out* for many happy years. She was kind to us and made us a very close family. The short excerpt from the book that follows tells it all. Even though a seasoned sailor in a Springer Spaniel suit plays the minor role in the episode, it might be worth repeating since the NOD was also involved.

In the passage Rog portrays the initial sail of *Over And Out.*

"... We joined Jimbo in the small cockpit. I raised the main into the southeast breeze, OG swung us around toward the opening in the rocks and gave us a shove. Marie hoisted the jib and we were underway! Clear of the bottom, we dropped the centerboard and headed for Fox Island. Hap was gone, but I am certain that the island recognized our distinctive silhouette.

The launching crew along with a host of other rowdy sailors, gathered on our front lawn watching us tack around the island. The orange ball attached to our mooring began to grow larger as we smartly came about for the final tack home. It was decided that the captain would make a full stop landing, at which time Marie would pick up the painter, secure it to the mooring cleat and casually return to the cockpit to help with lowering the sails, exactly as we had done so many times with Old Dad.

The off shore breeze had freshened and, of course, was gusty. To impress the pilots on the beach, I lined up with the imaginary runway, slacked the main just a little, sent the crew forward and prepared to make a standard full stop landing. Suddenly, I realized that the new machine was considerably faster than Old Dad. *We were on final, hotter than hell with no flaps or brakes.*

Okay, I'll take a wave-off. Everyone will understand. Before I could relay my wave-off message forward, Marie had the painter in hand. My emergency luff-up measure coincided with Marie's screaming entry into the water. The response from the grandstand was loud and clear.

"I'll take it around again and drop the jib. Don't go away," I yelled to Marie.

Away from the mooring and out of earshot, I luffed-up and dropped the jib- right on top of Jimbo who had moved up to Marie's station on the bow. I turned on final approach again slowed her down to a crawl and watched Jimbo try to get out from under the jib. Treading water and holding the bitter end of the painter high above her head, Marie yelled, "Let the main sheet go and grab this when you get close enough."

Jimbo found his way out from under the jib and leaped into the arms of his Marie. The painter disappeared. More applause from the stands.

"What the hell, over," I muttered to the fastest boat in the world, sheeted-up and sailed off to plan my third approach strategy.

Another roar from the stands. This time it was for OG who had launched the dingy, rescued Marie and Jimbo, and was rowing out to assist Over And Out.

Executing precision stalls with a one-design machine in a gusty breeze is the direct function of the "time in type" axiom. However, the low time captain, sans crew, accepted the challenge composed and determined. He must prove his skills and unravel the potentially disastrous predicament.

I maneuvered the craft as close to the wind as possible, hoping that the rescue vessel would understand my tactics. OG acknowledged and held his course. Over And Out *came alongside smartly, luffed-up and stalled. Marie held us apart and OG eased aboard* Over And Out. *Marie took command of the rescue vessel as we sheeted-up to get steerage way. No response from the stands. Finally, I asked OG, "What did Al have to say about all that?"*

Not much, OG answered. "Something like, I hope that he doesn't wreck the damn thing before I get a ride in it." We both laughed and headed for the mooring.

The final approach was slow and easy. The stands responded as usual. All I could say in my defense was, "Boy this thing is fast!"

Marie and Jimbo showered and joined the party. I found them sitting on the sea wall next to Al, quietly studying Over And Out *swinging peacefully from her mooring. I slipped in beside them and eased the tension with, "Al, how'd you scribe that perfect waterline?"*

"Just like I do on the quahog skiffs," he replied.

Must be a trade secret, I thought to myself. I took his empty mug and went off to get him another beer."

Al Potter was indeed a Swamp Yankee. Nothing was wasted, particularly words.

Life with my sailing parents became more demanding and, I must say, much more interesting. Not only did they ask me to endure countless hours in the tiny cockpit of the NOD, but they made friends with every boat that sailed past the house.

I will always remember the happy times aboard *Sea Shanty.* She was a gaff-rigged 50-foot fishing schooner built in Nova Scotia. Bill Johnson (another U.S. Navy commander) was stationed in that neck of the woods and bought her. He and his Navy friend Ed turned her into an unsophisticated but rugged yacht. Most of her worn and rusted gear was replaced with materials from a boat salvage yard. Her engine came from a wrecked taxi; the half civilian, half-Navy galley produced meals fit for any king. And my bunk was perfect.

I looked forward to the long trips on *Sea Shanty*. When all the busy work of getting underway was done, I would request to be relieved from my duty station and make my way down the nice wide ladder to the main salon, make a routine check for something to eat, and jump up on my bunk. Soon I would hear the clatter of the sails being raised. The engine was shut down and the helmsman would set just the right heel to make my bunk the most comfortable bed in the world. In reality I did not have an assigned bunk, but Bill's bunk was the biggest and very handy to the ladder. He never complained and I was very careful not to mess it up.

Sea Shanty was the perfect boat for me. The walkways were wide enough for a Springer, there were lots of places on deck to enjoy a quick nap in the sun with a friend, and the old schooner was a feeder! (U.S. Navy jargon.) We made some pretty nice ports at appropriate intervals for those who could not adapt to the complexity of a sea- going head, and often took time for a walk along a sandy beach. Bill and his *Sea Shanty* taught me a lot about the sea and about friendship.

A futile war transferred Bill away from us. The last time that we saw *Sea Shanty* she was tied-up at a dock on Pier 4 in Boston. Commander Bill returned alone. The war had changed him.

Well, There Goes Wickford

Jimbo And Friend Aboard Sea Shanty

Lunch Time Aboard Sea Shanty

Sea legs at last!

Boy! This Is A Long Watch

CHAPTER SEVEN

A Field day...

Sailing was a big part of my life by the sea, but when summer changed into fall we headed for the woods or some out-of-the-way quiet place at the end of a dirt road.   And I did get a rucksack strapped to my back.   Marie and Rog brought the contraption home from L.L Bean long before my time.   It was red

Can't we take a short break?

in color and almost matched my liver colored hair, and was small but large enough to carry a fair size lunch and a towel for drying after a swim. Marie redesigned the strap arrangement to provide a snug fit without interfering with routine relief stops. The rucksack has become sort of a status symbol. Other dogs in town sport fancy little plaid jackets advertising their heritage in a canine clan that doesn't exist, but my rucksack sets me apart from the fakers. I share the load. When Marie or Rog take it from my special hook in the closet I know that it is time for a nice walk. And besides, it gets a lot of laughs...

Our walks in Rhode Island and Connecticut sometime start from Nooseneck Hill Road (Route 3). We follow the Appalachian Mountain Club yellow markers along the ledges to Yawgoog Pond, take a lunch break, change to the blue markers in Connecticut, take a Snicker/dog biscuit break, and then backtrack to the car. Everyone is tired when we pile into the car, especially ole Jimbo. They don't seem to realize that I leave the trail many times and easily double or triple their mileage. But, then again, they never make me drive home.

The best walks are with Marie's father in the woods around the Quabbin Reservoir. John has walked just about every trail and road in the area. Rog grew up in a little western Massachusetts town called Dana. Since it was located within the boundaries of the Quabbin watershed, the Chapmans and their relations were forced to leave in 1936. It is fun to walk in from Gate 40 along the old Greenwich Dana Road to Skinner Hill Road, which passed Rog'sgrandfather's farm on Deadman's Curve. The farm house was perched on a hill looking west toward the Swift River valley. The cold spring that constantly filled a soapstone tank in the kitchen is still running. The old stoneware overflow pipe that runs under the road to the barn is still flowing. Of course, there are no longer cows and horses to water and their barn is gone, but it is nice to listen to Rog relive his childhood.

When there is time, we would walk into Dana center. We followed an old road past the site where Nellie Shattuck's house used to stand, then across the brook to the field where Rog's family lived. I forgot about my rucksack and had a great swim in the brook. Fortunately, we had taken our lunch break up at the farm. I shook off most of the brook and sat down between Marie and Rog, who were involved in a story about the little house where Rog grew up.

Rog's dad worked for the U.S. Post Office and sorted the mail on the night train from Springfield to Boston. During one of his overnight trips, a violent thunderstorm bore down on Dana and their home. His mother gathered Rog and his brother Dick into the kitchen to wait out the storm. All at once, a lightning bolt struck the chimney and split the cast iron kitchen stove right down the middle. With Dick cradled in one arm and Rog hanging on to her other hand, she ran out the kitchen door, across the barely visible bridge and straight into her best friend's kitchen. Nellie lived alone and welcomed her guests with open arms. The storm passed, but the frightened group spent the night together. If I had been around at the time, I would have spent

Nancy, Jimbo and John Having a Field Day

The Best Walks Are With John And The Other Dogs

Heidi Looking For Jimbo on Rome Point, Rhode Island

the night under the bed!

When we walk with Marie's dad John, I have to be at my best. He trains hunting dogs—English Pointers and Setters-and I expect that he looks down his nose at breeds like mine. Once in a while, I'll point a pheasant or a grouse just to let him know that we are a hunting breed too. Deep down, I think that he likes me. One day I'll make him tell me so...

Occasionally, John will include me on one of his field training sessions with the other dogs. John modifies the shelf above the back seat of his Fords to allow plenty of air into the trunk, which is where bird dogs must ride. Imagine, four dogs crammed into a space designed to store a spare tire and a bag or two of groceries. The other dogs just jump up into the trunk, but I have trained John to assist me by lifting my back feet to get me up and into the trunk. It would not be polite for me to repeat the words that he utters as I fall on top of the others and he slams the trunk door. In the beginning, the other dogs gave me dirty looks and ostracized me, but in time they respected my

After A Long Day In The Field A Short Nap Is In Order.

valor. I look forward to the field trips, and I must say I do pretty well with the bird hunting thing, in spite of the shotgun blasts. Of course, I was not allowed to compete in the field trials with the big boys. But that's their world, and they may never know the challenge of a seagull chase at great speed in the soft white sand along miles of a secluded beach. It beats romping all afternoon in a field of tall grass filled with ticks, to find a bloody old bird. And I can go for a quick swim in the ocean when I run out of seagulls. The only bad part is the cold shower when we get home.

Rog and I are early risers. Nearly every morning we have our special time together walking along the shoreline from our house out to a spit of land that separates Narragansett Bay from Bissels Cove. The jaunt out to the Hummocks and back is about two miles round trip, and it keeps us lean and mean. I'm okay after a couple of dog bones but Rog has to have his cup of black coffee before the rest of his day begins. Often when Rog is out to sea, Marie will walk with me in the morning. It's really nice. Marie finds sea flowers, and I chase anything that moves. Living by the sea is a nice life. I wish I knew where the runt ended up. I hope he is having as much fun as I am. Perhaps one day we will see each other again.

CHAPTER EIGHT

Father Jimbo

This morning, during breakfast, I overheard a telephone conversation between Marie and the girl down on the waterfront who has the other Springer on the plat. It appeared to me that they are arranging some sort of meeting for me with that rather stuck-up bitch. Perhaps I should clear this with Nemo. He should be showing up pretty soon. I'll get out in the yard and wait for him. Oh, good. Here he comes now.

"Hi, Nemo. We have to talk."

"What's the problem, Jimbo?"

How do I explain something that I really don't understand?

"Nemo, today I heard Marie and the girl down on Seaview Avenue planning some sort of a special meeting for me and that long-legged Springer that lives with her."

"Special? What does that mean?"

"I really don't know. But there was a lot of talk about the bitch being ready by next week."

"Okay kid, she'll be in heat and ready for breeding," Nemo chuckles and continues.

Father Jimbo

"I guess they want you to be the father."

"What do I know about being a father? Only yesterday, I was a child! What do I to have do?"

"Well, it's sort of like learning to lift your leg, but it will be a lot more fun. And I won't be able to help you. You'll be on your own once they put you together, but I'll explain the basic procedure. We better find a nice quiet place to talk."

"How about over under the maple?"

"Okay, but keep your voice down. This sort of thing is private in the people world. The thing that we do so naturally is secret and very discreetly performed within the confines of their bedrooms. If someone arrives, cool it. Who knows just how much of our language people really understand? We don't want the whole neighborhood to know about your upcoming escapade."

"Okay, Okay! But what do I do?"

"Nothing special, really. In our world, everything comes along naturally. All you have to do is wait and follow your nose. When she is ready, you answer the call to duty and before you know it you are on the way to fatherhood. Not to worry. You're not the first to sire a litter of puppies or be left alone with a bitch in heat."

"Are you sure that everything will happen naturally?"

"Of course. But chances are that they will close the two of you in the garage and wait for you to complete your assignment. If there is a problem, just check the north window. I'll be standing by with the appropriate paw signals."

"Okay, but I'm not sure that I want to produce a bunch of long-legged, skinny Springers. After all, I am proud of my heritage and would like to pick out my partner."

"But Jimbo, you're living in a people controlled world. Just live with it and have a ball. Maybe it won't "take" this time. Next time, turn on your commutation switch and talk it over with Rog. I know he will understand your desire to continue the genealogy and locate just the right partner for you."

In spite of all the anxiety, the bitch down the road produced six nice, normal, AKC- sanctioned puppies.   And Nemo was right. It was fun becoming a father.

CHAPTER NINE

Trick or treat...

Fall is the best time of year for me. The hot, humid summer days have given way to crystal-clear illusory autumn afternoons that seem to bring Prudence and Patience Islands right into our front yard.

Marie and I are so alike. A simple walk along the shoreline among the tall sea grass or a field filled with a gaggle of Canada geese taking a lunch break is all that we need. But I must say that I wish, just once, that she didn't insist on making me heel when we come upon the geese. Surely she knows that I could never catch one! But I'd love to try. I bet if John was along he would send me right into the middle of the flock.

As I reread certain paragraphs of this presumably simple narrative it occurs to me that a great deal is lost, or added, in the translation. What kind of a canine author would use a word like "illusory?" And, I am quite certain that few will know that Prudence and Patience Islands are located in Narragansett Bay. Or, for that matter, realize that Narragansett Bay is in Rhode Island. That's the price you pay for having to use a ghost writer. Now back to fall and all its splendor.

New Kid on the Plat

Trick Or Treat

Halloween arrives in fall. A holiday defined by Mr. Webster as, "short for *All Hallow Even:* October 31 observed with merrymaking and the playing of pranks by children during the evening..." Initially, the *pranks* part was very difficult for me. Modern-day Halloweeners have moved up from marking windows with soap and throwing eggs at the front door to destroying everything in sight. Dogs are an easy mark for todays pranksters with their spray paint, gunny sacks, and fireworks.

My first Halloween night will remain with me forever. I was captured by a gang of older kids and thrown into our garage along with a package of lighted fireworks. Of course, Rog and Marie came to rescue me, but it ruined my cahnces of becoming a renowned bird hunter.

Oh, yes, we were talking about splendor. Few Springer Spaniels dress up for Halloween unless, of course, they live with people like my folks. After the fireworks episode, Marie decided that it would be better for me to dress up and blend in with the merrymaking children. "Who would recognize a Springer Spaniel if he was dressed up like a little boy with long hair?" she explained.

Everything moved along on schedule and a few days before Halloween Mister Jimbo made his final trip to the fitting room. Attired in Marie's tailor-made "man suit," I made my entrance into the world of make believe. From a pair of youngsters' white Levis, a small plaid shirt, a rather oversize raccoon hat and my little red rucksack, she fashioned a universal walk or-beg outfit that has served me well for several Halloween nights. After a few moments of special education and practice sessions of sit up-and-beg in my new outfit, I was able to bilk most neighborhood treaters into at least one dog bone or some other choice goodie.

Our trick-or-treat routine was as follows. Marie or Rog would knock on someone's door and slip back into the shadows. I would take their place, just sit up, and give them the standard trick-or-treat portrayal. Most would do a routine double-take, leave for a moment and return with something nice to put into my rucksack. Some of the more serious in-house treaters who had been tricking since late afternoon would grab a candy bar from their swaying basket, slip it into my rucksack, and mumble something like, "Must be a new kid on the plat." Rather than expose our scheme, Marie might say in her best falsetto voice, "Thank you..." Once, I added a soft bark in *my* best falsetto voice that prompted a loud belch and a rapid slam of the door.

When we did Nemo's house, Charlie and Jackie played along with the whole idea and Nemo just sat there like he didn't know me. I thought to myself, "Either this get-up really fooled them or they have a secret Halloween trick hiding in the wings."

Just one stop netted a trick instead of treat. Someone had neatly packaged a rare and very ripe road apple and discreetly placed it in my rucksack! Since there are absolutely no horses residing on our plat, I am reasonably certain that a U.S. Navy commander made a covert visit to a stable.

CHAPTER TEN

The MG TD and the roastbeef...

When I recall some of the events that have transpired throughout my years of living by the sea, I have to smile and wonder what would have happened if I had been handed the life of a pampered pet living in the splendor of a plush mansion with my private kennel and a butler to bring me my supper. How differently my autobiography would read! Rides in country viewed from the back seat of a chauffeured limousine, perhaps a secret cabin tucked away in the mountains of a distant country, my own stateroom on a fancy yacht or a cozy room on the 25th floor of a modern hotel in the center of New York City.   None of these things can compare to the fun I have had on Wild Goose Point, a nondescript jog in the West Passage shoreline of Narragansett Bay.

We were nearing the end of the spring of my second year with my new parents when it was decided that it was time for new screens for both outside doors. Rog was assigned the task of rescreening each door. He finished the front door panel and passed it to Marie for installation. I watched the operation from the rug in front of the fireplace. Rog called to tell Marie that the back door was ready for installation. She finished, stood back to enjoy the fruit of her labor, opened the door, and joined Rog at the back door. Since I was still in the house and all the activity was outside, I decided to join the action crew. Normally, I would just back off a few paces, bump the door, and it would open. This time, it didn't. I dove right through the new front door screen. With mixed emotions, I slipped in next to Marie where she was installing the rear door panel.

"Hey ! I thought that you were inside!" For a moment, I thought that I saw a light come on above Marie's head as she started running toward the front door.

"Damn you Jimbo Chapman...You've ruined the brand new nylon screen!"

Marie grabbed me by the collar, assisted me back through the hole in the screen, shook her finger at me and said, "You get under the kitchen table and don't come out until I tell you to!"

From my newly assigned station, I witnessed a hushed conversation and, I think, some audible smiles, between Marie and Rog who were standing by the back stoop.

Marie said in a loud voice, "Let's go for a swim. We'll leave him in the house."

That's not fair! How was I to know that Rog had replaced the worn latches on both screen doors. I lost control, jumped through the back door screen and joined the swimmers.

"I guess he used the front door again," Rog said.

Somewhere along the line, Rog decided that Marie should have an MG TD. There was much ado about the 1952 English classic that was scheduled for arrival next Saturday. Exactly as planned, the shiny red two-seater was delivered. Marie slipped into the driver's seat, listened to instructions from the delivery driver and backed out of the driveway.

Rog leaned against the split rail fence and said, "What do you think, Jimbo? Does she like it ?"

Marie returned, down shifted as programmed, stopped, and opened the other door.

"Okay you guys, it's your turn. Get in."

Jimbo's Very Own English Sports Car

I, of course had to take a back seat, even though there really wasn't one, and Rog folded into the other seat.

"I love it!" Marie sang with the sound of the little engine.

I loved it, too! What could be more perfect than an English Springer Spaniel cruising around Wickford in a rare English sports car. Talk about class!

By fall, the TD and Marie and Jimbo were part of the Wickford scene. Marie would park in front of the drug store, hurry across the road and into Ryan's Market while I guarded our little red classic from the passenger seat. I'm not a mean guy, but nobody should touch the TD. Usually, the "standard sore paw, lip turned-up routine" would suffice but, on occasion, I would have to show a few more teeth and put the hair up on my back, lest some kid would fingerprint the whole hood. In time, I was able to sort out the real TD lovers and let them inspect my classic beauty until they were happy. Not one dog ever lifted his leg on our whitewalls while I was on my duty station!

I must admit that there were times when I had to question the mechanical attributes of our English chariot. One afternoon, Marie and I were returning from a shopping trip in Wickford. All at once a rather spirited cold front settled upon us. As the wind increased in speed the soft top filled with air, and one of the fastenings designed to secure the front of the convertible top reached the limit of its holding power. Marie managed to grasp the leading edge of the top with her left hand. Then came the rain! Fortunately, the inoperable electrical windshield wipers were rigged with a manual handle which Marie operated intermittently with her right hand. As we roared over the little white bridge across Bissel Cove, I took my eyes off the road just long enough to witness a feat only an MG lover would appreciate. Holding onto the top with one hand, working the windshield wiper with the other and steering with her knee, Marie was taking us home at about 40 miles an hour. She let go of everything, slipped into the garage and said, "How's that for driving, Mister Jimbo?" I wonder if she noticed my smile?

Occasionally, I used to get into trouble around the plat. I recall one rather humorous occasion involving the "Dirty Doctor" who summered in the log cabin on the corner of our road. Dr. Lou was a professor of agronomy at the University of Massachusetts up in Amherst. Thus, we gave him an appropriate nickname.

Dr. Lou spent a good portion of a Saturday morning preparing a fine standing rib beef roast for the oven. Finally, the roast was placed into the oven and in due time it began to fill the neighborhood with its distinctive aroma. I may not be the finest hunter on the plat, but I do have a good nose. The doctor, rocking away on the porch and absorbed in the *Providence Journal*, never heard the screen door close after I tactfully pushed it into the kitchen. There it was! Brown and steaming on the counter, just waiting to be eaten. Stretching my body to its maximum limit, I was able to place my front paws just over the edge of the counter top. Little did I know that the carving set was there until it came crashing to the floor. In desperation, I ran to the door only to find that I could not get out. Soon Dr. Lou rushed into the kitchen from another entry and started to shout and swear at me. There was nothing for me to do but snarl and fend him off. The maneuver appeared to be very effective. Dr. Lou burst back though the door and the next thing I heard was, "Marie? This is Lou. Your GD dog is holed-up in my kitchen guarding my roast beef and he won't let me near the damn thing! Get the hell over here and take him home!" The telephone receiver slammed back into place.

Marie arrived in great haste and rushed into the kitchen with Dr. Lou a step behind.

"Jimbo Chapman, what do you think you are doing?" Marie shouted.

Now isn't that just like a girl? What does it look like? I've staked my claim and am having a little fun with the doctor.

Marie pushed open the screen door, grabbed my collar and booted me out into the yard.

"Now you get home. I'll deal with you later!"

On the hasty trip down the back steps, I caught a glimpse of the two of them standing in the center of the kitchen with just a touch of a smile on their faces. On the way home, I wondered if they were still laughing or if Marie was catching hell for my shenanigans.

Months later, I was under the kitchen table pretending to sleep while Marie and Dr. Lou were talking gardening. The doctor paused, asked for another beer and said, "You know, Marie, I've told that story about Jimbo and the beef roast a thousand times. I don't think that the little SOB would have bitten me, so when he came back the next day I gave him the trimmings."

Big mouth! All this time she was convinced that her scolding had paid off. Now you ruined it. (And, in my case, SOB is an actuality, not a swear word.)

As the years passed and the Dirty Doctor and I mellowed, the two of us established a mutual understanding. He tried not to let me know that we were more than just friends and I learned to tolerate his gruff but honest personality.

One warm fall afternoon, the quieting sea breeze was soothing the doctor into his routine nap session. Sprawled out on his favorite Adirondack lawn chair, the *Providence Journal* spread out in his lap and his eyes nearly closed, he was the perfect Normal Rockwell picture of vacation.

I was just finishing my rounds and thought that it might be nice to join him. Careful not to disturb his reverie, I sat down next to him. He opened his eyes for a few moments, rested his hand on my head and said, "Hello, Jimbo. You're a good dog, but sometimes you piss too close to the well."

I smiled, closed my eyes and joined him in the unknown.

CHAPTER ELEVEN

Doctor Kind...

The most feared occasion for just about every dog is a trip to the vet. The prospect of having some guy, (or girl, for that matter) push you here, bend you there, pry open your mouth or any other place they have to stick something— and all that on a cold and slippery stainless steel table. It is not a happy evening. Unless you happen to have a friend like Dr. Kaplan.

As the years piled up, I picked up an allergy to something. Rog and Marie took me to every specialist known in the veterinarian community. Each prescribed a new and wonderful medicine to relieve my itching. All failed to help for more than a day or so. Finally, a kind old vet told us about Dr. Kaplan.

"He's a large animal vet, but he loves all creatures and he might help you if you talk with him."

It took some talking but Marie persuaded Dr. Kaplan to see me at 6:30 that night. I had reached a new low and I wondered if anyone or anything could help me. But what's one more vet?

We arrived at his office sad and weary. Dr. Kaplan entered the waiting room and called us into the examining room. Even though I was not at my best, I studied his kind face. Convinced that he was really interested in helping us, I relaxed and listened to Marie and Rog explain my problem and closed my eyes. Many minutes must have passed before I returned to the group standing over me.

"There. I gave him a shot of cortisone. It should give him some relief. It is difficult to treat this sort of ailment but I've had a fair amount of success with other long haired dogs with similar symptons," Dr. Kaplan said to Marie and Rog.

"Thank you, Dr. Kaplan. We'll let you know how he does," Marie replied.

"If it's going to work, you will know within a couple of days or sooner."

Dr. Kaplan gently helped me to my feet. Marie lifted me from the table and carried me to the car. Once again, I accepted the warmth of my wonderful blanket and waited for Marie to radiate some lap heat. Rog started the car and I closed my eyes again. I awoke on the kitchen couch still wrapped in my blanket. Everything around me was crystal clear. I wanted to get up from the couch and jump with joy. Marie and Rog were sitting beside me waiting for me to wake up.

"Rog, I think he is awake. Look how alert he is! Do you think the cortisone could work that fast?" Marie asked.

"Perhaps it does. Let's leave him alone for a while. I'll make a pot of coffee," Rog answered.

Well, I guess that I had better show them I'm all better. I'll just stand up, stretch, and jump off the couch. Wow! I did it. Boy, do I feel great. That Dr. Kaplan really knows his business.

"Rog! Look at your Jimbo!" Marie cried.

"Marie, he's like a new dog! That stuff really works. I'll call Dr. Kaplan." Marie said.

After all the nonsense about, "No, he really shouldn't be in the salt water..." and "Don't let him eat this and that..." — one shot of cortisone and I'm all better!

Of course, the cortisone was effective for only a few weeks, but it was great while it lasted. When I began to hurt again, off we would go to see Doctor Kind. And it was back to running on the beach in Narragansett, chasing squirrels , hanging around with my friend Nemo, and watching Marie smile again. I actually looked forward to visiting with Dr. Kaplan. Rog was so happy that he made an eleven by fourteen portrait of me and gave it to him. It hangs in the waiting room, and if we have to wait to see Dr. Kaplan I sneak a quick look at the other patients to see if they recognize me. I know that one fluffy little poodle bitch knew who I was but she just turned her head the other way when she caught me checking her out.

CHAPTER TWELVE

Jimbo! I think that I heard you speak to me...

The noon sun cast a perfect shadow for me to take a short nap under the maple. A southerly breeze swept a path across my favorite rest area as I settled into the cool grass. My mind started to fill up with pleasant thoughts and stopped at a picture of Marie's face.

I must find a way to communicate with her. There is so much I have to tell her. Talking with Rog is good, but Marie and I have a special bond that could become so much more if only I could talk to her. I'll just close my eyes and think about it.

How do I make the initial contact with her psychological thinking process? Rog was easy. I just slipped into a void someplace in his think tank and turned on the switch. Perhaps I should take a look at the bonding element. What do Marie and I really have in common?

We both like dogs. We love the simple things: the woods, the sea, snow, rain, walking, swimming, red meat, and Rog. Let's start with Rog. I'll just stay here and wait for Marie to come by. Something is working already. Here she comes!

"Jimbo, it looks like you have found the best place to spend your busy day," she says softly, sitting down beside me.

In a few moments I sneak a quick one eye look, only to find that she appears to be off in another world completely oblivious to all that surrounds her. Now is the time.

"Marie, I had a nice chat with Rog this morning," I silently transmitt into the unknown.

"Jimbo Chapman! I think that I just heard you speak to me! Marie softly divulged. And, what do you mean that you had a chat with Rog?"

"We have been communicating for some time now."

"I can't believe this!" Marie utters to me and the maple tree.

"Marie, think how great it will be to be able to tell each other everything. But I'm not too sure that we should tell Rog about this until the time is right."

"Okay. But it's not going to be easy."

She leaned up against the rugged bark of the maple, closed her eyes, and waited for me to take her beyond the mystic door we had just opened.

"But, Marie, I must tell Nemo. He is such a good friend and there have been so many times I have wished I could have explained to him what you guys think."

We sat there for an hour or more— not a single word was spoken. I know there are few, man or beast, who would believe this obscure excerpt from my strange life. Even Nemo would have trouble accepting such a fable, but it really happened!

Marie reached over, put her hand on my sleepy head and said, "Are we dreaming all this, Jimbo?"

Before I could compose an appropriate reply, Marie was gone.

CHAPTER THIRTEEN

We didn't mean to hurt him lady...

On occasion, my wanderlust would take me beyond the limits of my assigned territory. Late one afternoon I ventured south along the waterfront roadway. After passing a few houses, I happened upon a porch door that had been opened to let in some of the cool sea breeze. Since all was quiet, I decided to investigate.

"Well, hello big dog. Come on in and join us," uttered the musty darkness.

When my eyes began to adjust to the surroundings, I saw two partially attired young men sitting on a dilapidated sofa. Their white uniforms, neatly draped across an old wooden bench, quickly revealed their profession.

"There's room for one more right here in the middle," said the one on the left.

I hesitated for a moment then slowly walked in their direction.

"We are enjoying an after-work beer," added the sailor on the right.

I'll just sit here for a little while if you don't mind, I

thought to myself and sat down in front of them.

"How about a pretzel? They're fresh and you need the salt in this weather," he said.

They seem to be okay guys and I do like pretzels. I'll move in some so that they can reach me if they are serious about the pretzel.

"I guess that the redhead has taught you to be careful of strangers. Not a bad idea but we're okay, Jimbo."

How in the world does he know my name? I never saw these guys before. And who does he think he is, calling Marie the "redhead"!

Lefty breaks a pretzel in half and holds it out for me to try. I've heard that sailors are crafty and probably not too kind to animals, so I'll play it cool and wait for him to drop it on the floor.

"I guess you don't trust me!" he replies, and eats the pretzel.

"We had a Springer back on the farm and he was pretty smart. Probably he doesn't like pretzels and is waiting for us to break out the hot dogs," the one on the right reasons.

"He can wait until hell freezes over before I give him a hot dog," counters the one on the left.

"I forgot all about the hot dogs. Let's cook up a few instead of making supper," Mr. Right suggests.

"Okay. But that dog isn't getting any hot dogs!" Lefty insists.

Mr. Right leaves for the kitchen and I am alone with Mr. Mean. Perhaps I should high tail it out of here before I get in trouble.

"The hot dogs are underway. I dropped one of them on the floor so I'll give it to Jimbo."

"You dropped one of yours. You can do whatever you want with it!" Lefty says and smiles to me.

"He's easy."

Mr. Right returns to the kitchen. But where is the hot dog? Guess I had better wait around for a few more minutes.

"Jimbo, don't get me wrong. I like dogs or I wouldn't let you in here. I just have to be strong with Dean. He's too kind. If I don't discipline him he would give everything away."

Well, that's one name, Dean. Rhymes with Mean, you know. Dean and Mean, what a team.

"The dogs are ready. Want another beer?" came from the kitchen.

"Yeh. Better bring in a saucer and one for Jimbo. Hot dogs are nothing without a beer."

I'm not having any beer! Just bring the hot dog.

Dean arrives from the kitchen with a tray. Two plates with three hot dogs on each one, three bottles of beer and another plate with two hot dogs.

" How come Jimbo gets two hot dogs? You didn't drop another one did you?" Mr. Mean asks.

"No. You donated one of yours."

"If you can't handle it, I'll cook up another batch when these are gone."

The two plates with three hot dogs and the beer bottles are arranged on the orange crate coffee table in front of the sofa. The saucer and my plate with two hot dogs are set on the floor on the other side of the table. Dean opens one of the beers and pours some beer in my saucer. For just a moment the room was silent. Neither of the guys moved and I think they closed their eyes. Someone says, " Amen." Then they start to eat.

Boy, that yellow stuff that they put on the rolls is pretty strong. My mouth is burning! Maybe I will have to drink some of their beer just to cool down a bit.

"Hey, Jimbo! Wake up. I think that the redhead is calling you. You better not go back by the waterfront. Go out front and through the yards." Dean whispered in my ear.

"He might be in big trouble. He's been gone more than four hours!" Dean said.

"We'll be in big trouble if she ever finds out!" Mr. Mean replied.

I took their advice, made my way home through the yards and thumped on the back door.

"Jimbo Chapman, where have you been? We have been looking for you all night!" the redhead said.

"We have to go to Owen's for supper. We'll be home around seven. You'll have to wait until we return for your supper, if you get any at all," she added, and they rushed out.

Who needs supper? All I want to do is get some rest. Now where is their bedroom? Oh, ya. Over there.

Why can't I get up on the bed? Perhaps I should move back a little and get a running start. Wow! Missed it completely. Too low. Better go back more. This should be okay. Now I must shoot higher.

Too high! Ended up on the floor again. But I have the range now.

There! Right on target. I'll just close my eyes until they get home.

"Rog. I wonder where Jimbo is?"

"Probably on our bed. We left the door open you know. I'll check."

"Come here and take a look at your Jimbo."

"He looks so comfortable. I hate to wake him, Rog."

"You better. He's probably hungry."

"Jimbo. Wake up!"

"Not you, too. Why can't they let me sleep? Leave me alone!"

"Did you hear that, Rog?"

"Yes. How did you know that I can talk with him?"

"Because I talk with him, too!"

"This is scary! We better wake him up."

"Leave me alone, I said! Don't touch me or I'll bite you!"

"Rog! He just snapped at me! I think that he is sick. Should I call Jackie? She's a Navy nurse."

"No. Let's just put him on the floor for awhile and see how it goes."

"I said, don't touch me. And I mean it. I want to sleep!"

"I don't know, Marie. We stayed at OG's pretty long. It might be too late to call Jackie."

"I'm going to call her, anyway!"

"Jackie. This is Marie. Sorry to call you so late but I think Jimbo is very sick. Would you please come down?"

"Of course. I'll be right down."

"What happened to him, Marie?" Jackie asked.

"He was gone all afternoon. When he finally came home, we were late for supper at OG's. So we left him here."

"Let me look at him."

Now they are sending in the U.S. Navy. I'm just too tired to fight it again. I'll let her have her way. Perhaps then they will let me sleep!

"Marie. Help me roll him over."

Now they want to roll me over. Okay, but be careful. Oh, I'm sorry. I know that it's not nice to burp when you have company.

"Marie! Did you smell his breath? Your GD dog is drunk! Let him sleep it off!"

Jackie turned on her heel and stomped out of the house.

"I'm sorry, guys. Please help me onto the floor so you can have your bed." Before I could close my eyes I dropped off into tomorrow.

I spent most of the following day tucked under the kitchen table. Nothing seemed to work. Walking was difficult and the very thought of food upset my stomach. Marie wouldn't talk to me and Nemo ignored me completely. As a matter of fact, she and Nemo went for a walk without even asking if I wanted to join them. Well, at least I have two new friends down on the waterfront who will be nice to me.

"Rog. Jimbo is gone again. I let him out around four o'clock and he hasn't returned!" Marie said when Rog returned from the Naval base.

"We better take a walk around the plat to look for him," Rog replied.

"You stay here. I think that I can find him."

Marie rushed through the back door, let it slam closed, and ran cross lots to the road along the waterfront. When she approached the house where the sailors lived, she burst through the porch door that was ajar.

Jimbo was sitting on the sofa between the two sailors. The threesome was well into a standard after-work snack.

"So this is where you are!" Marie shouted. She grabbed me by the collar and shoved me out the door.

"Now. You get home! I'll settle with you later!"

She returned to the sofa and said, "What kind of men are you? Getting a dog drunk is about as low as you can get. If I catch him near this house again you guys will find out what an Irish temper looks like!" She took a deep breath and added, "Why don't you just go to a bar like real sailors do? Pick a fight with a Marine or start a brawl, but leave my dog alone!"

Marie slammed the door as she left. I was waiting on the porch.

"I told you to go home!"

As we headed down the road we could hear the sailors calling out behind us, "We didn't mean to hurt him, lady."

Cap'n Jimbo Chapman 1955-1969

EPILOGUE

Cap'n Jimbo Chapman brought to us fourteen years of friendship, love, laughter and just a few moments of sadness. God gave us a very special gift that we learned to cherish more each day. His adventures and cavalier character became part of our precocious lifestyle. We adjusted to him and he to us. Our worlds, although vastly different in nature, seem to meld into an unexaminable symmetry. Soon our little white house on Wild Goose Point became more than just a place to live. No one ever mentioned it, but suddenly a family lived there.

Hundreds of sailboats large and small, have sailed past the house where Jimbo lived. He walked the decks of some and endured countless hours tucked away in *Over And Out,* his very own sailboat. A rugged sailor, steadfast friend, and humble humorist, Jimbo Chapman filled his life with people. We are so fortunate to have been among them.

ABOUT THE AUTHOR

Liver and white English Springer Spaniel, *Cap'n Jimbo (S-779196)* resulted from the union of sire, *Out Of Bounds Driver (S-429291)* and dam, *Carvelyn Ruthie's Run (S-538138)*. He arrived in Perkinsville, Vermont November 27, 1955.

Cap'n Jimbo joined Roger and Marie Chapman of Wild Goose Point, Hamilton, Rhode Island, on March 16, 1956. Since he was from a long line of champions it was decided that Cap'n Jimbo should continue the tradition. On April 5, 1959, he was introduced to the world of champions at a show in Cranston, Rhode Island. By the end of that infamous day, Cap'n Jimbo had won three ribbons, *First Prize, Best Of Opposite Sex*, and a dubious blue ribbon labeled *Winners.* The Champion and his two exhausted handlers drove back to Hamilton in silence.

The sparkle in Jimbo's eyes was gone. For five days he moped around the house, ate very little and completely ignored his best friend Nemo. Cap'n Jimbo's search for fame and fortune in show business vanished when one of the judges ran his talented hand across Jimbo's powerful chest and declared, " His swimming muscles are much too over developed." But sir, he is a water spaniel!

Cap'n Jimbo thought that he was human... And, most of us went along with it.

ABOUT THE GHOST WRITER

Since Cap'n Jimbo was somewhat computer illiterate, he elected to enlist the services of a local translator who owned a personal computer. Enter Roger Chapman. Roger spoke Jimbo's language, labored countless hours over his Macintosh and lived in the neighborhood. A hasty review of his chosen biographer's qualifications revealed the following.

Twenty-five years of writing technical reports and articles as a civilian field engineer assigned to military projects. Continous writing, mostly on the blackboard, during a twelve year tenure in the classroom of a vocational shool and a lengthly thesis for a master degree. Photographs and/or articles have appeared in *Yankee, Maine Coast Fisherman,(presently National Fisherman), The Standard Time, The Providence Journal* and his photo-narrative book, *Over And Out* , was published in 1997. The ghost has come out of the closet and is currently writing another photo-narrative, *Romancing The Ski.*